To Sarah 8/29/2013
With love from Mama

Children are a gift from the Lord;
they are a reward from him.
Psalm 127:3

A 3-minute forever book

EAT YOUR PEAS®

Daughter

By Cheryl and Mom Karpen

Illustrated by Sandy Fougner

There are only
two lasting bequests we can hope
to give our children.
One of these is roots,
the other is wings.

Henry Ward Beecher

At the heart
of this little book
is a promise.

It's a promise
from me to you
and
it goes like this...

If you ever need
someone to talk to
(really talk to),
someone who will listen
(really listen),
to your worries,
your joys,
and your dreams...

I promise
to stop what I'm doing,
give you my undivided attention,
open my heart, and listen.

I promise to be there for you
day and night,
through times of hilarity and times of heartache.

In the meantime,
there are some things
I want to tell you~

like how important you are to me,
how I only want the best for you
and how I wish you joy in life.

Dazzling, irrepressible joy!

I can't wait!

Go ahead and turn the pages.

(Read often for maximum smiles and hugs!)

Here goes...

When you were
first placed in my arms,

I had no idea
what wonders awaited me.

This heart of mine
is bigger than you can imagine
and you have filled it with
unimaginable
joy.

Just think...

I was remembering things
about you
before you were able to remember
things for yourself.

Anything you'd like to know?

FIRST WORDS ♥ FIRST DAY OF SCHOOL ♥ FIRST SMILE ♥ FIRST BIRTHDAY ♥ FIRST LOVE ♥ FIRST DRAWING ♥ FIRST TRIP ♥ FIRST FOODS ♥ FIRST STEPS ♥

Beauty comes wrapped in many packages:

a smile,

an intelligent mind,

an act of kindness,

a loving heart.

You are so beautiful.

May I always know when
to give you room to wander
and wings to fly.

Life is filled with
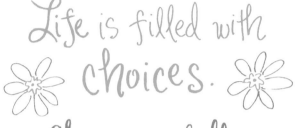 choices.

Choose carefully.

Always
pray for, wait for, work for, reach for,
what will make you
feel alive and complete in life.

Keep a dream in your pocket
and faith in your heart.

Anything is possible!

Begin each day
with thoughts
that bring out the best
in you.

Today I will...

Yes, I can...

I am
grateful for...

No challenge in life is so big that we can't handle it together.

I'll always be there for you.

Even in the deepest heartache,
there is comfort in
humor.

May we always know how
to make each other smile
and give each other
reasons to hope.

I'm keeping you close in my heart
and near in my prayers.

Whether on the sidelines or in my heart, I will always be the one cheering the loudest for you.

I can't help but smile every time

I think of the person you've become.

I count you among
my blessings every day.

For I know the plans I have for you," declares the LORD, "plans to prosper you and not to harm you, plans to give you hope and a future.
Jeremiah 29:11

Sometimes life
doesn't go as planned
and
not getting what we want
becomes a blessing
in disguise.

There is a plan for you.
Have faith.

Be patient, and most of all...
Believe.

Be kind.

Be really kind and gentle with yourself.

For good health and a strong spirit,
repeat 10 times daily!

I am lovable.

I am loving.

I am loved.

I will always
believe
in you.

God gave me a daughter
to brighten up my world.

To this day, it is full of sunshine
because of you.

There will be times in our life
when we simply will not agree
or understand one another.

And that's okay.

One day we may even laugh about it.

Never forget that
home
is the permanent address of the heart.

The door is always open for you.

Every time
you pick up this little book,
consider yourself

hugged.

And cherished too.

Have faith always.
Sing boldly.
Embrace your authentic self.
Be generous.
Listen. Love. Smile. Forgive.
Cultivate lasting friendships.
Live compassionately.
And by all means... have fun!

Why Peas?

She was a vibrant, dazzling young woman with a promising future. Yet, at sixteen, her world felt sad and hopeless.

Though I was living over 1800 miles away, I wanted to let this very special young person in my life know that I would be there for her, across the miles and through the darkness. I wanted her to know she could call me any time, at any hour, and I would be there for her. And I wanted to give her a piece of my heart that she could take with her anywhere—a reminder that she was loved.

Really loved.

Her name is Maddy, and she was the inspiration for my first book in the Eat Your Peas series, *Eat Your Peas for Young Adults*. At the very beginning of her book, I made a place to write in my phone number so she would know I was serious about being available. And right beside the phone number, I put my promise to listen—truly listen—whenever that call came.

Soon after the book was published, people began to ask me if I had the same promise and affirmation for adults. It was then that I realized it isn't just young people who need to be reminded of how truly special they are. We all do.

Today, Maddy is thriving and giving hope to others in her life. I like to think that, in some way, I and my book were part of helping her achieve that. If someone has given you this book, it means *you are a pretty amazing person to them*, and they wanted to let you know. Take it to heart.

Believe it, and remind yourself often.

Wishing you peas and plenty of joy,

P.S. My mama always said, "Eat your peas! They're good for you." The pages of this book are filled with nutrients for your heart. They're simply good for you too!

If this book has touched your life,
we'd love to hear your story.

Please send it to:
mystory@eatyourpeas.com
or mail it to:
Gently Spoken
PO Box 245
Anoka, MN 55303

With gratitude...

To my mother, Julia Karpen
I have invited my mother to co-author
Eat Your Peas for Daughters. Not only is she a wonderful
mother to three grateful daughters, this woman also happens to be
one of the most remarkable individuals I have ever known.

I am not the only one who thinks so. My sisters and I
are honored to have shared our Mom with other adopted daughters
over the years—girls and women whose own mothers
have passed on or live too far away for a hug.

I like to think of us as Julia's garden...living proof this
amazing woman makes things grow wherever she goes. Planting hope.
Pruning doubt. Cultivating courage and creativity. We are stronger,
straighter...more resilient because of you. Thanks Mom...from all your girls.

To illustrator, Sandy Fougner
You plant LOVE on every page with your
spirited artistry. And it shows.

To editor, Suzanne Foust
Sometimes I send you weeds and you turn them
into beautiful flowers. Amazing.

-CK

About the author "Eat Your Peas"

A self-proclaimed dreamer, Cheryl
spends her time imagining and creating
between the historic river town of Anoka, Minnesota
and the seaside village of Islamorada, Florida.

An effervescent speaker, Cheryl brings inspiration,
insight, and humor to corporations,
professional organizations, and churches.
Learn more about her at www.cherylkarpen.com

About the illustrator

Sandy Fougner artfully weaves
a love for design, illustration and
interiors with being a wife
and mother of three sons.

Other books by Cheryl Karpen

The Eat Your Peas® Collection

now available:

Eat Your Peas® for Mom
Eat Your Peas® Faithfully

New titles sprouting up in Summer 2011

Eat Your Peas® Girlfriend
Eat Your Peas® Faithfully, Love Mom
To Let You Know I Care

Eat Your Peas® Daughter

Cover design by Koechel Peterson & Associates
Minneapolis, MN

ISBN-13: 978-1-4041-8983-6

Printed in China

11 12 13 14 15 [RRD] 5 4 3 2 1

www.thomasnelson.com